QUIET MOMENTS WITH GOD SIXTY DAY DEVOTIONAL

Connie C. Smithson

authorHOUSE®

AuthorHouse™
1663 Liberty Drive
Bloomington, IN 47403
www.authorhouse.com
Phone: 1 (800) 839-8640

Published by AuthorHouse 05/01/2020

ISBN: 978-1-7283-6074-4 (sc)
ISBN: 978-1-7283-6073-7 (e)

Print information available on the last page.

This book is printed on acid-free paper.

DEDICATION

To my sweet Isla Dare. Out of all the ways God has blessed me, you are by far, the greatest blessing of all. Your smile lights up the room and brings Joy unspeakable to my heart. It is my prayer that you will let the Holy Spirit guide and lead you through this life. Always seek His face and His will first. On those days when you're feeling discouraged, I pray you find words of encouragement in Gods word, as well as the words contained in this devotional.

Love You sweet girl,
"Gammy"

INTRODUCTION

As I go through each day, I find that more people are contacting me looking for an encouraging word. God laid it on my heart to write this Sixty-day devotional based on His word and what Jesus died for us all to experience as we go through life.

So many Christians are living a life of depression, despair and discouragement. This book is intended to encourage people and help them to grow in their walk with God. The Holy Spirit is our deliverer, our healer, our strength, our refuge, and our hope. He is all that we need and is the answer to all of life's problems, no matter how minor or major. At the end of each Chapter is a page for notes. I encourage everyone who reads this book to study the scriptures and apply them to their daily life as they grow in their faith and continue their walk with God.

Connie C. Smithson

DAY

1

"And He said, take now your only son, Isaac, whom you love, and go into the land of Moriah; and offer him there for a Burnt Offering upon one of the mountains which I will tell you of."

- Gen. 22: 2

We all know the story of Abraham and Sarah and how Abraham at age one hundred and Sarah age ninety were promised a son by God. Against all odds Sarah bore Isaac who Abraham adored. Some years later, Abraham, who is now well over One Hundred years old is being asked by God to offer his only son, Isaac, as a burnt offering, a sacrifice. This experience would reveal to Abraham the means by which God would redeem humanity—by the death of His only son, Jesus Christ.

Abraham after much prayer and questioning whether

he was hearing from the Lord, determined that it was the Lord and in obedience traveled for three days before arriving to the place where God would have him stop and build an altar. Laying his only son down to be sacrificed, Abraham took the wood of the Burnt Offering, and laid it upon Isaac, with fire in one hand and a knife in the other, Abraham proceeded, as Isaac questioned where the lamb was for the burnt offering.

As Abraham stretched forth his hand and took the knife to slay Isaac, an Angel of the Lord called unto him, stopping him. Abraham lifting his eyes looked, and saw a ram caught in a thicket by his horns. Abraham went and took the ram and offered him up as a burnt offering instead of his son.

How many times has God given us a task to complete that we really did not want to tackle? How many times has God ask us to sacrifice something dear to us for the sake of drawing closer to Him? There are many lessons that we can learn from this short story about Abraham and Isaac. One of them is obedience. When God gives us an assignment, we are to do it with His help. If it is of God and from God, He will provide all that we need to complete it. If God requires us to sacrifice those things that are precious to us in order to carry out the task at hand, then we must out of obedience to him be willing to sacrifice whatever it is, so that His plan may go forward and His will, not ours be done.

I challenge you today to examine your heart and think of the things in your life that are keeping you from spending quality time with God. Maybe it is something God has been dealing with you on, that you need to lay down, so that you can draw closer in relationship to Him.

NOTES

DAY

2

"And he said, Hearken you, all Judah, and you inhabitants of Jerusalem, and thou king Jehoshaphat, Thus says the Lord unto you, Be not afraid nor dismayed by reason of this great multitude; for the battle is not yours, but Gods."

-II Chronicles 20:15

Jehoshaphat, like us, had a character flaw of making wrong choices. He also went through trials and tribulation, just as we do. However, it is through Jehoshaphat that we can learn how to have confidence in God during a crisis—not confidence in ourselves. Jehoshaphat's crisis was a great multitude coming against him from beyond the sea. This enemy coalition coming after Jehoshaphat meant his life and entire kingdom were on the brink of extinction. If ever there was a time to panic and react without thinking, it was now! Jehoshaphat did just the opposite. He called a national prayer meeting and encouraged the people to trust God in the face of this overwhelming crisis.

They, as Jehoshaphat, ask and won the war by prayer alone, without swinging a single sword! Likewise, when we go through a crisis, we should follow this same example and not fight the battle on our terms, but on God's terms. If we try to take matters into our own hands, we will fail, but if we let God fight the battle we will win.

Jehoshaphat could have reacted with panic; he also could have had anger toward God. He had just instituted reforms to bring the nation back to the Lord. It would have been easy for Jehoshaphat to have said "*what kind of deal is this, God? I tried to bring the nation back to you!*" However, he did not do this, but rather turned to God in prayer.

We have all tried to follow God and been hit with difficult trials in the process. Trials that left us feeling angry, sorry for ourselves and complaining to others. What we should always do is cry out to God in prayer and trust him to fight for us. After all, the battle was won at Calvary and the outcome has not changed, we win! The victory is ours!

NOTES

DAY 3

"So, Moses brought Israel from the red sea, and they went out into the wilderness of Shur; and they went three days in the wilderness and found no water. And when they came to Marah, they could not drink of the waters of Marah, for they were bitter; therefore, the name of it was called Marah. And the people murmured against Moses, saying, what shall we drink? And he cried unto the Lord; and the Lord showed him a tree, which when he had cast into the waters, the waters were made sweet."

-Exodus 15:22-25

The Lord showed Moses a tree, which was a type of the Cross. When Moses grabbed the tree and put it into the bitter waters of Marah, they were made sweet.

It was out of obedience to what the Lord was telling Moses to do and by Faith that Moses grabbed the tree and cast it into the water. First came the problem, then came obedience which followed an expression of Faith and then came the victory. If Moses had just looked at the tree and not grabbed it, the water would not have been made sweet and there would have been no victory. Likewise, when we have a problem God wants us to by Faith, be obedient to the leading of the Holy Spirit in our circumstances and grab the tree, stay grounded in the Cross, so we to, can experience victory in our lives.

Oftentimes we are more like the children of Israel and we forget where God has brought us from and resort to murmuring and complaining followed by asking God why? As you face trials and tribulation, do you grab the tree and hold on, wait on God, follow His lead? Or are you more like the children of Israel, quick to murmur, complain and try to figure it all out on your own? Be encouraged today to wait on God for the answers you are seeking and when He tells you to grab the tree, be obedient and by Faith grab it and wait for the victory.

NOTES

DAY

4

"And the Lord said, I have surely seen the affliction of my people which are in Egypt and have heard their cry by reason of their taskmasters; for I know their sorrows."

-Exodus3:7

The children of Israel faced many afflictions. As God's children we also face afflictions. Every trial that comes our way as a child of God is either caused or allowed by him for a purpose. There are many reasons for why God allows trials to come upon us. For instance, when things are going well for us, we do not pray the way we do when we are in the wilderness. God wants to hear from us constantly and at times he wants us quiet so we can hear from him.

God desires a relationship with us and like all relationships it requires talking and listening. Another reason God allows affliction is to test our faith. God wants to teach us dependence on him, he wants to show us his provision as we go through, so by teaching us dependence and showing us how he will provide, our faith is built.

At times, God allows affliction in our lives to prepare us for the call he has on our life. God wants to move us from our comfort zone; remove things and/or people from our life that may be hindering what he is trying to accomplish through us. He breaks us down, so he can build us back up, to what He wants us to be.

Finally, God allows affliction to see how we will respond. He allows things to get as bad as they can at times, to show us our weakness. What is in us will ultimately come out of us and while God knows what is on the inside of us, we do not always know. He allows the affliction to intensify and when it does, we see things like envy, jealousy, bitterness, hate, resentment, selfishness and unforgiveness come to the surface. Once we recognize the "junk" that is not of God, then we can turn to God for deliverance and he shows us his delivering power. What is afflicting you today? More important, what is God trying to teach you through the affliction?

Be encouraged today to allow God to search your heart, as you seek His face during the trial you are in and ask Him what life lesson, He would have you to learn. In His faithfulness He will answer.

NOTES

DAY 5

"Bring you all the tithes into the storehouse, and there may be meat in My House, and prove Me now herewith, says the Lord of Hosts, if I will not open you the windows of Heaven, and pour you out a Blessing, that there shall not be room enough to receive it."

-Malachi 3:10

The Lord is challenging us as His children to give and prove him regarding the rewards of tithing which will be super abundance. We are to pay our tithes to the work of God. Tithe means "one tenth." Are you giving one tenth of your income to God first and with a joyful heart? Or do you tip the Lord by giving just a little and not what you can give?

God expects us to be good stewards of the money that he blesses us with. In Malachi 3:8-9, it reads: *will a man rob God? Yet you have robbed Me. But you say, Wherein, have we robbed You? In tithes and offerings. (9) You are cursed with a curse: for you have robbed Me, even this whole nation.* For us to use all our money for personal gain is robbery of that which rightfully belongs to God.

The choice is entirely up to us. Blessings or curses? May we all be quick to obey the Lord, knowing that he will provide all our needs according to His riches in Glory.

Be encouraged today to begin tithing, giving God what is His first and extra as a love offering when the opportunity presents itself. You can't out give God, so give abundantly, with a joyful heart and watch what God will do in your life.

NOTES

DAY 6

"Stand fast therefore in the liberty where with Christ has made us free and be not entangled again with the yoke of bondage."

-Galatians 5:1

When a man or woman is arrested they are captured and become a captive, they are handcuffed, shackled and the officer holds the key to unlock the handcuffs and shackles, however, if he or she is on their way to serving a prison sentence, although, the handcuffs and shackles are unlocked and removed, they are still held captive as they are put into a prison cell.

The key that unlocked the handcuffs and shackles are replaced with another key that unlocks and locks the prison cell door. They remain a captive. Likewise, when a person is in bondage to sin, they are in a spiritual prison with Satan holding the key that only locks the door. They are a captive to the powers of darkness, with no key to unlock the door. There is only one way out and that way is to cry out to God in brokenness, and surrender. He will be faithful to hear, and he has made a way out through the blood shed of his son at Calvary. Jesus paid the price to free us from the powers of sin and darkness.

Jesus, name above all names and freedom from sin. At the mention of His name freedom reigns; call his name and be free today in Jesus name.

Be encouraged today to surrender to God all that the enemy is using to hold you in bondage. Call on the name of Jesus and He will meet you where you are and free you from the powers of darkness.

NOTES

DAY 7

"In my Father's house are many mansions, if it were not so I would have told you. I go to prepare a place for you and if I go to prepare a place for you, I will come again and receive you unto myself; that where I am, there you may be also."

-John 14: 2-3

As we go through life, we prepare for life events that will take place along the journey. When a couple announces their engagement, wedding preparations are made, when there is the announcement of a pregnancy, the new parents begin to plan for the day the baby will arrive. In addition, we plan for things such as, what school we will go to, what career we will work in, retirement and old age. We tend to prepare for everything except the most important event of our life, and that is when we draw our last breath. Why is this the most important event of our life? Because it is at that moment when we draw our last breath, that our future begins. It is at that moment we will either enter Heaven, that place God has prepared for us or Hell a place God prepared for the Devil and his angels. In order to make Heaven your future home, you must accept the Lord Jesus Christ into your heart and have a relationship with him. He is the Way, Truth and Life. My question to you today is simple. Have you prepared for your future?

If your answer is no, be encouraged today to skip ahead to Day sixty of this book where the sinner's prayer is written and give your heart to Christ. Your future depends on it.

NOTES

DAY 8

"For the Lord Himself shall descend from Heaven with a shout, with the voice of the Archangel, and with the trump of God: and the dead in Christ shall rise first. Then we which are alive and remain shall be caught (raptured) up together with them in the clouds to meet the Lord in the air and so shall we ever be with the Lord."

-I Thessalonians 4:16-17

You and I will be the alive and remaining talked about in this scripture, that is how close we are to the rapture of the Church taking place. At any moment we could be raptured out of this world and into Heaven to be with our Lord and Savior. Have you ever thought of what you will be doing at the exact moment the trump of God sounds and Jesus comes for you?

I challenge you today to think about it. What will you be caught in the act of doing when Jesus comes? Will you be worshipping him in your Church, Home or car? Will you be helping a friend, neighbor or someone in need, possibly even a stranger? Or will you be gossiping or doing some act of sin that isn't pleasing to God? This is something that we should all ponder as we are living in the very last of the last days here on Earth. Caught in the act. What will you be doing?

Be encouraged today to live your life saying and doing those things which are pleasing to God. Live your life today as if Jesus is on His way, after all, today could be the day He comes for us all!

NOTES

DAY

9

"You are of God, little children, and have overcome them: because greater is He who is in you, than he who is in the world."

-I John 4:4

As a child of God, we all go through hard times and walk through the valley of trouble. We all have enemies and unfortunately our enemies are often those close to us, our friends, family and neighbors. Whatever the trouble and whomever the enemy is in your life, know that there is one greater living on the inside of you, walking with you and fighting the battle for you.

When you grow weak, God will revive you. When the wrath of your enemies comes against you, God will stretch forth His hand against them. His power is greater than the wrath of your enemies and the powers of darkness. Stay grounded in your faith, focused on God and look away from the circumstances that try to hinder you. God has everything under control.

Be encouraged today to stay focused on God rather than your circumstances and what others say or think about you.

NOTES

DAY 10

"For He said, I have heard you in a time accepted, and in the day of Salvation have I succoured you: Behold, now is the accepted time; behold, now is the day of salvation."

-II Corinthians 6:2

As Christians we should have a burden for loss souls. Everywhere we go the light of Jesus should penetrate through us for others to see. We need to be telling others what God has done in our life. If we are saved, then we have a testimony that needs to be shared. For some, perhaps even you, it is not easy to walk up to a stranger and start a conversation about anything, especially Jesus and how he died for them. While talking to strangers about Jesus may not be within your comfort zone, every one of us has an obligation to tell others about His saving grace.

Pray and ask God to bring you out of your comfort

zone and to give you a boldness so whether you are in the workplace, the grocery store, school or at a Doctor's appointment, you will have the courage to reach out to others.

The time for salvation is now, the time is now to get people saved, and the time is now for us to play our part in God's kingdom, the time is now. I challenge you as you go out today to be a witness to someone about Jesus and tell them how his blood was shed, so they can be set free from the bondage of sin and spared an eternal Hell.

NOTES

DAY 11

"Thus says the Lord God unto these bones; Behold, I will cause breath to enter into you, and you shall live."

-Ezekiel 37:5

Paul said, *"For the preaching of the cross is to them who perish foolishness; but unto us which are saved, it is the power of God" (II Corinthians 1:18).* The power Paul is speaking of is the Holy Spirit, and without the Holy Spirit, saved individuals are nothing more than a pile of dry bones in need of the breath of life.

Without the Holy Spirit man is spiritually dead. If man is dead on the inside, then he is simply taking up space within the church, and as a result the church is also dead, because the congregation is the church, not the building. In the book of Ezekiel, only God could cause the dry bones to live again. The dry bones, even after being covered with flesh and skin, were dead, until the wind was told to blow upon them, then and only then, were they restored to life.

The wind was an emblem of the Spirit of God and represented His quickening power. The same holds true for Christians today. People accept Jesus Christ into their lives, and they believe in the sacrifice, the price Jesus paid at Calvary; but they reject the infilling of the Holy Spirit. Although, they are saved and on their way to Heaven, they are dead spiritually. Why? Because they have not received the power afforded to them through the cross.

Be encouraged today to seek God for the baptism with the Holy Spirit. He desires to fill you.

NOTES

DAY 12

"When Jesus came into the coasts of Caesarea Philippi, He asked his disciples, saying, whom do men say that I the son of man am?"

-Matthew 16:13

Jesus in a meeting with his disciples asked them *"Whom do men say that I am?"* They responded by saying, *"some say that you are John the Baptist, some Elijah, and others Jeremiah or one of the other prophets."* Jesus then asked them, *"Whom do you say that I am?"* The disciples did not respond, suggesting that they agreed with what men were saying and that Jesus was merely just another prophet. Simon Peter, however, answered him saying *"you are the son of the living God."* Jesus replied, *"Simon for flesh and blood have not revealed it unto you, but my father who is in Heaven."*

Peter's response to this question was one of Faith and an

illustration of what it means to have a true relationship with God, therefore being led by the Holy Spirit.

If you had walked with Jesus and watched him perform miracle after miracle and he ask you, *"Whom do you say that I am?"* Would your response have been one of Faith like Peter or one of unbelief like the other disciples? Who is Jesus Christ? He is the son of the living God, He is the source of all blessings, He is more than a man, He is the tried foundation of the Church, and He is a redeemer for all of humanity. Who is Jesus Christ? He is all that we need.

NOTES

DAY 13

"Train up a child in the way he should go: And when he is old, he will not depart from it."

-Proverbs 22:6

Since the start of the decade suicides among teens has doubled. The cause of the suicides is said to be multiple issues, including, but not limited to, high anxiety, mental illness, bullying and negative family situations.

In reality, Satan is robbing us of our children and our future. We, as a society seem to know the problem, as well as the cause; however, it is the solution that we have gotten wrong. Our youth do not need a Psychologist, Psychiatrist, or another bottle of pills. What they need is Jesus Christ as a foundation in their life. The laying of this foundation begins at home with the parents, as it is the parents responsibility to bring them to church and the church's responsibility to provide them with the truth of God's word, a word that they can grow in and carry with them as they face daily challenges at school and abroad.

Our youth may not know what the future has in store for them, but one thing is for certain, they are our future. If their parents and church family do not commit to the building of a foundation in Jesus Christ, the way, truth and life, Satan will be sure to live up to his promise to kill, steal and destroy.

I encourage you to pray for our youth today as well as their parents. Be a positive influence in the life a young person. If their parents aren't attending church, invite them to your church. If their parents reject your invitation, offer to take their children.

Let the light of Christ shine through you as you strive to make a difference in the lives of our youth and parents train your children in the way they should go, so that, when they are older they will have a foundation that holds and will not depart from it.

NOTES

DAY 14

"Fear you not, for I am with you: be not dismayed, For I am your God: I will strengthen you, yes, I will help you; yea, I will uphold you with the right hand of my righteousness."

-Isaiah 41:10

God is saying to us in this verse that He is with us. When we go through times of trouble, when life comes at us hard and the enemy brings us to our lowest point. God has promised to pick us up, put us back on our feet and bring us out. He alone is our strength, our help, our righteousness. He is all that we need to make it through.

As you go through the trials of life that we all face, remember that God is holding you up with his right hand, his hand of power and because he is holding you, you aren't going to crumble, you aren't going to be destroyed, but rather, you will succeed, prosper and come out of the trial victorious. We serve a faithful God that has only the best plan for us. Stand on his promises today, get into his word, seek his face in prayer and know that whatever you are going through, you will come out victorious!

NOTES

DAY 15

"Will you not revive us again: That your people may rejoice in you."

-Psalm 85:6

The word revive means to make someone or something strong, healthy, or active again, to bring life back. In America, our Church and our personal lives we are in desperate need for reviving—spiritual renewing. Why? Because life happens. Every day the world, the flesh and Satan beat until we are spiritually lethargic.

The church needs revival so we may come together corporately and worship all in one accord, allowing the Holy Spirit to move and bring a new awareness of God's Holiness, our sinfulness, and His abundant Grace.

A true revival cannot be planned. Advertising *"Revival this week"* does not mean there will be a true revival. True revival happens when people come together, the Holy Spirit shows up and lives are transformed forever.

In Hebrews 10:25 it says, "*Not forsaking the assembling of ourselves together, as the manner of some is, but exhorting one another and so much the more, as you see the day approaching.*" We are to come together and create a joyful, reverent atmosphere, an atmosphere where the Holy Spirit takes the lead and we follow.

Why do we need revival? To renew our hearts and minds. We need revival to recommit ourselves to the Lord; We need revival to allow the Lord to cleanse us and finally, we need revival so that corporately we can celebrate Gods abundant Grace that extends to all who will draw near to Him through the blood of Christ.

Be encouraged today to pray for a great revival to break out across our Nation, with an outpouring of Gods spirit, a Harvest of souls and miracles of healing and deliverance like we have never seen.

NOTES

DAY

16

"When you pass through the water, I will be with you; and through the rivers, they shall not overflow you: when you walk through the fire, you shall not be burned; neither shall the flame kindle you."

-Isaiah 43:2

Throughout Israel's history this verse has proven to be truth. This scripture is a prophecy that not only applies to Israel but also to Christians. As we go through this life, we are going to have problems. The key word in this scripture is *"through."*

God promises to bring us *through* the waters, *through* the rivers and He says when we walk *through* the fire. God is telling us that as we face the problems of this life, He is all that we need to make it through.

When we step into the water (when we go into a

problem) He will be with us. When we go through the rivers (the problem begins to worsen) He will be with us and when we walk through the fire (the problem gets as bad as it can, with no end in sight) the flame will not kindle upon us, because He is with us!

No matter what you are going through today, be encouraged, knowing that our Heavenly Father is with you, carrying you as you step into the water, go through the river, and trample through the fire. No problem is too big for our God!

NOTES

DAY 17

"And He said, So is the Kingdom of God, as if a man should cast seed into the ground; and should sleep, and rise night and day, and the seed should spring and grow up, he knows not how. For the earth brings forth fruit of herself; first the blade, then the ear, after that the full corn in the ear. But when the fruit is brought forth, immediately he puts in the sickle, because the harvest is come."

-Mark 4:26-29

The parable of the seed deals with the responsibility of believers to spread the Gospel. When the word is sown properly then the outcome will be effective. When a farmer plants a crop, first, the ground has to be broken and prepared for the seed, after which comes the planting of the seed.

For the seed to grow it must go through a process. The

seed will require water, fertilizer and the light of the sun during the growth process. Once that seed is a plant, at times weeds will sprout up around it and try to stop the success of full growth. The farmer sprays chemical to kill the weeds and then the plant can finish growing to its full potential thereby producing the harvest.

The seed, now a plant full of fruit, cotton, beans or whatever it bears can be harvested to go out into the world and serve its purpose. Likewise, as Christians, we must also be prepared for what God has called us to do. At times God allows events in our lives to break us and free us from self, so He plants us in a position of stillness to give us one on one time with Him. During this time God fills us with more of His Spirit, followed by His word and then He brings us into a deeper prayer life.

As we are growing in Christ, often the enemy will attack and try to stop what God is doing. It is important to remember during this time of attack that God has given us the weapons of prayer and His word. Get them out and stay in the fight! After God is finished with us, we find that we have grown Spiritually, and are now ready to do what God has for us to do. We are ready to experience victory and receive the harvest. Stay in the fight! The VICTORY is worth it!

NOTES

DAY 18

"Then shall the Righteous shine forth as the sun in the Kingdom of their Father. Who has ears to hear, let him hear."

-Matthew 13:43

This scripture refers to the coming Kingdom Age. However, as I meditated on it, God revealed to me that before we come to the knowledge of Gods saving Grace and get saved, we are unrighteous and living in darkness. After receiving the Lord Jesus Christ into our hearts and lives, we are made righteous through the blood of the Lamb, the darkness passes away, as we step into the light.

When the sun sets at the end of a day, it gets dark. This reminds me of fallen man. When the sun rises, the light comes, this reminds me of man saved by Grace. Man can only be saved, if he or she hears the word. It is Gods will that every man and woman hear the true word of God. I challenge you today to go out and tell someone about Jesus Christ and how He died on Calvary's Cross for them to be saved. Be obedient to the word of God so that ALL who have ears to hear will hear the gospel of Jesus Christ and come out of the darkness into the light.

NOTES

DAY 19

"Then came Peter to Him, and said, Lord how often shall my brother sin against me, and I forgive him? Till seven times? Jesus said unto him, I say not unto you, until seven times: but until seventy times seven."

-Matthew 18:21-22

Jesus is telling us that we are to forgive those who do us wrong as many times as they ask. For as long as we live, family, friends, our church family, and people in general are going to say or do something to hurt, offend us or both.

At times they may come to us and ask for our forgiveness, other times, they may act like nothing was ever done to bring us harm, go about their life and never ask us for forgiveness. Whether they ask or not, it is imperative that we forgive them.

When we choose to hold a grudge and not forgive,

it doesn't hurt the one who caused us grief, it hurts us. Ultimately, what they did to us will fester and before we realize it, a Spirit of resentment, bitterness, revenge and strife will settle in, and we will find ourselves in bondage. Meaning, those Spirits will be controlling us, stealing our peace and joy.

Regardless of what someone says or does to us, we must forgive and ask God to remove the sting of the memories that we have of what they did. We can forgive but forgetting is another battle. However, God can make it so that when that memory of what they did comes to our mind, it will not have a negative impact on us.

I am sure that as you read this, you are thinking of someone who has wronged you. Perhaps, someone that you have not forgiven. Ask God today to help you forgive that person and to take away the sting of the memory so that it will torment you no more. He will be faithful to hear you and to answer your prayer.

NOTES

DAY 20

"For where two or three are gathered together in my name, there am I in the midst of them."

-Matthew 18:20

This scripture is simple to understand. Where there are at least two people joined together, God promises to be there with them. In todays world everything is fast pace, and everyone is too involved with their cell phones and other computer devices to pay attention to the people around them. Unfortunately, this also applies to the home.

Parents are too busy for children, and children are too busy for parents. Instead of spending time having dinner together, having conversation or just simply enjoying the company of one another, everyone is running in a different direction.

Parents should be a positive influence on their children, guiding then and leading them according to Gods word. I want to encourage parents, as well as children, to put down their cell phones.

Plan an evening when everyone can come together, get out the Bible and have a Bible Study in your home. After all, where two or three gather God promises to be there, so whether your home consist of a new couple starting out or you are a family of five, God will be in your midst. The example you set for your children today, will be the example they set for their children tomorrow.

NOTES

DAY 21

"You have heard that it has been said, You shall love your neighbor, and hate your enemy. But I say unto you, Love your enemies, bless them who curse you, do good to them who hate you, and pray for them which despitefully use you, and persecute you."

-Matthew 5: 43-44

God commands us to not only forgive our enemies, but to love them. When people talk about us, use us, or mistreat us in any way, we are to love them. How do we do this? We do this by praying for them, and when what you really want to do is give them a piece of your mind, pay them a compliment. Bless them with a gift or a note of encouragement.

In our own strength we do not have what it takes to show this kind of love to those who despitefully use us; therefore, it is imperative that we turn to God for guidance and strength. It is through the power of the Holy Spirit that hurts can be healed and we can move forward in forgiving and loving the people who cause us pain.

I challenge you today to send a note, buy a small gift, pay a compliment or encourage someone who has mistreated you and watch as God blesses you in return.

NOTES

DAY 22

"After this manner therefore pray you: Our Father who is in Heaven, Hallowed be your name. Your Kingdom come, your will be done in Earth, as it is in Heaven. Give us this day our daily bread and forgive us our debts, as we forgive our debtors. And lead us not into temptation, but deliver us from evil: For yours is the Kingdom and the power and the glory, forever, Amen."

-Matthew 6:9-13

The above scripture is known as the model prayer. It is an outline of how God says we should pray. We should start our prayers by reverencing our Heavenly Father, not Christ or the Holy Spirit. We must follow this by praising and worshipping God with thanksgiving for saving us, delivering us, healing us, baptizing us with the Holy Spirit and all the many ways He blesses us daily. Next, we should not only ask Him to provide our daily bread, what we have need of, but to also meet the needs of our family, friends, church family, our Country, Israel, and to forgive us of our sins, and help us to forgive those who have cursed us and done us wrong.

We should ask Him to lead us and guide us by His precious Spirit away from temptation, deliver us from the evil one that comes against us constantly. God is all power and can handle what we cannot. Remember, the model prayer is just that. A model of how we should pray, rather than a ritual that we read out loud on a special occasion or use as a routine in our church services.

NOTES

DAY

23

"That you put off concerning the former conversation the old man, which is corrupt according to the deceitful lusts; and be renewed in the spirit of your mind; and that you put on the new man, which after God is created in righteousness and true holiness."

-Ephesians 4:22-24

The apostle Paul in this part of the epistle to the Ephesians is addressing the lifestyle that as believers we are to exhibit. Paul is explaining to the Ephesians how their former lifestyle, the way they lived before coming to Christ, should be different from the way they conduct themselves after coming to Christ—there should be a change.

The moment we are saved the sin nature is broken. Sin no longer has dominion over us. Before we were saved and living in the world, the sin nature dominated us. We did whatever we wanted, whenever we wanted, however we wanted and didn't give thought to the wrong being committed or the lasting effect it would have on us.

Once we got saved, we became a new creation in Christ Jesus, the old man has passed away. We do not talk the same, walk the same or look the same. There is or should be a lasting change in us that only comes from accepting Christ into our hearts.

NOTES

DAY 24

"Know you not, that so many of us as were baptized into Jesus Christ; were baptized into His death? Therefore, we are buried with Him by baptism into death: that like as Christ was raised up from the dead by the glory of the Father, even so we also should walk in newness of life. For if we have been planted together in the likeness of His death, we shall be also in the likeness of His resurrection."

-Romans 6:3-5

As Christians we are united with Christ, we died with Him, were buried with Him and are resurrected with Him—we are in Christ. The instant we are saved, the Holy Spirit goes to work on us. This is a work that will continue until we take our last breath here on Earth.

While the old man passes away and the new man raises

up, there are still things about us that must be dealt with, changes that need to be made. Our biggest and greatest problem is self. Jesus died at Calvary's cross to save us not only from sin but from self. If we aren't careful, after getting saved, we will get our eyes off what Christ did for us and wants to do in us and onto ourselves, what we can do and the way we want things done. Our will takes precedence over Gods will for our lives.

It is important that we remember who we are in Christ Jesus and keep our focus on Him, so that we may continuously be Christ-centered and not self-centered.

NOTES

DAY 25

"Humble yourselves therefore under the mighty hand of God, that He may exalt you in due time: casting all your care upon Him; for He careth for you."

-I Peter 5:6-7

Peter is writing this epistle to a group of Christians who are suffering great persecution. He is encouraging them to keep their faith, while at the same time warning them about false teachers and dealing with the commands concerning their conduct.

As Christians, how we live our lives in front of others is critical. When others see us and how we react to different situations, they should see us being a witness for Jesus—an example of who He is.

Jesus, although facing death on the cross, kept His faith in believing His Father would come through for Him.

Likewise, we should humble ourselves, believing God to come through for us in every situation we face, no matter how significant or insignificant it is.

Be encouraged today to let your light shine that others may see Christ in you and in all things, cast your cares upon Him who cares for you.

NOTES

DAY

26

"Trouble and anguish have taken hold on me: yet your commandments are my delights."

-Psalm119:143

As we go through life, we will face trouble. At times the problems we endure will be more difficult than at other times. Life is full of ups and downs, heartache and pain. Regardless of the magnitude of the problem, we should never forget that our help comes from the Lord.

He is always there for us to lean on and one of the ways we do that is by staying in His word. His word is our sword, our strength, our encouragement and it holds the answer to all of life's challenges, no matter how big or small.

Whatever the problem, do not let it discourage you and turn you away from Gods word, but rather let the problem carry you to Gods word and dig deeper into His word as you seek out the answers you are desperate for. Meditate on His word, letting it sink deep down inside of you and although the problem may remain, the anguish will begin to fade as the peace of God consumes you and the comforter comforts you.

Be encouraged today in whatever you are facing or may be facing by the end of the day, to get into Gods word and allow Him to guide you by His Spirit through the word, His word is truth and it is life, so let it lead you in the way that you should go. The answers will come and sooner than later, this too shall pass.

NOTES

DAY 27

"And he shewed me Joshua the high priest standing before the angel of the Lord, and Satan standing at his right hand to resist him. And the Lord said unto Satan, The Lord rebuke thee, O Satan; even the Lord that hath chosen Jerusalem rebuke thee: is not this the brand plucked out of the fire?"

-Zechariah 3:1-2

The Lord showed Zechariah that the true adversary to Israel was not the Samaritans or other heathen nations around them; their true adversary was Satan. The same is true for us. Our true adversary is Satan. However, as we can see in reading this scripture the Lord our God is with us, He hasn't left us, nor has He forsaken us. Second, we see in this passage that God is more powerful than Satan; Third, we see that God is in control, always has been, is today and always will be; Fourth, we see that God has chosen us, He didn't have to choose us, but He did, because He loves us; and fifth, we see that we are like a brand plucked out of the fire. This is what the Lord told Satan and Israel to make them aware of what He had done for them.

Satan's plan for us was Hell's fire, which is what the fire in this passage is referring to. Satan's plan of destruction for us was destroyed when we accepted Jesus Christ as our Lord and savior. When we accepted Christ, we became the brand plucked out of the fire!

Let us all be encouraged today to give God glory, with a heart of thanksgiving, that He sent His only son, to not only die for our sins, but that we may be spared an eternity in that awful place called Hell.

NOTES

DAY

28

"And said, If thou will diligently hearken to the voice of the Lord thy God, and will do that which is right in his sight, and will give ear to his commandments, and keep all his statues, I will put none of these diseases upon you, which I have brought upon the Egyptians: for I am the Lord that health thee."

-Exodus 15:26

When Jesus died for us on Calvary's Cross, He not only died for our sins but for our healing. Many people believe that healing is only for the physical body, but that is far from the truth. Jesus died so that everything that is broken in our life could be put back together, not just our physical bodies. Getting saved is a game changer. We go from Satan having control over our lives, to Satan having to ask Gods permission to come near us. When he does gain Gods permission, we are promised by God that He will not allow more than we can bear to come upon us, oftentimes it is how God chooses to test our faith.

Sometimes this test may include sickness, but God is our healer. He has the final say. If you are sick in your body today, in a spiritual dry place, having problems in your family, marriage or facing a financial difficulty, remember Jesus died for you to be healed in EVERY area of your life. Be encouraged today to stay focused on Him and His healing power.

NOTES

DAY

29

"Fear not, you worm Jacob, and you men of Israel; I will help you, says the Lord, and your Redeemer, the Holy one of Israel."

-Isaiah 41:14

In this scripture the term "worm Jacob" could be replaced with "Lost Sinner" to represent us. Worm Jacob is used to help Israel recognize that their help comes from the Lord, not because they are good but because God is good.

The same holds true for us. We cannot do anything to earn Gods love or to cause God to help us. God doesn't love us, help us or bless us because we are good and deserve it. God loves us, helps us in times of trouble and blesses us because He is love and He is good.

Before we gave our heart and life to Christ we were lost, undone and in need of a Savior. God provided a way for us to be forgiven of our sins and set free from the powers of darkness through His son Jesus Christ, therefore we no longer are viewed by God as "worm Jacob" or "lost sinner." We can now be called son or daughter of God. We are a child of the most—high God and even as His child we cannot call ourselves good or deserving because we aren't, but He is forever good, forever faithful, forever there waiting to bless us with all that we need. Today I encourage you to humble yourself before the Lord and thank Him for his goodness, regardless of what we are. He is good.

NOTES

DAY 30

"Behold, I will make you a new sharp threshing instrument having teeth: you shall thresh the mountains, and beat them small, and shall make the hills of chaff."

-Isaiah 41:15

God promised Israel that He would not only sustain her but strengthen her to subdue her enemies. When people talk about us, raise up against us, and unjustly take advantage of us, God will give us the strength to stand against them.

As a child of God, we are not to let people intentionally take advantage of us or abuse us on any level. However, at the same time, when opposition comes, there is a way that we are to deal with the actions of other people, and it is not through retaliation. We are to show love to those who cause us pain and pray for them. If someone says something to you or about you that is hurtful or untrue, take it to the

Lord and ask Him to deal with them. Do not speak harshly to that person or talk about them behind their back, that makes you their equal verses who God says you should be in him.

I want to encourage you today to put a smile on your face and the next time that person crosses your path that has said or done something wrong to you or about you, pay them a compliment, do not ignore them, shake their hand and speak to them first. Let the love of Christ shine through you and watch how God will turn the circumstance around, working it all out for your good and Him to get the glory.

NOTES

DAY 31

"To everything there is a season, and a time to every purpose under the Heaven."

-Ecclesiastes 3:1

The above scripture continues by telling us that God has a time for all things. Scripture says, "*there is a time to be born, a time to die; a time to plant, and a time to pluck up that which is planted; a time to kill, and a time to heal; a time to break down, and a time to build up; a time to weep, and a time to laugh; a time to mourn, and a time to dance; a time to cast away stones, and a time to gather stones together; a time to embrace, and a time to refrain from embracing; a time to get, and a time to lose; a time to keep, and a time to cast away; a time to rend, and a time to sew; a time to keep silence, and a time to speak; a time to love, and a time to hate; a time of war, and a time of peace.*" The only way to understand the time God speaks of in these scriptures is to walk after the Spirit.

Gods timing is as important as His will. God wants us to do His will, in His way and in His timing.

After forty years in the wilderness, God appointed Moses to lead the children of Israel out of Egypt. Prior to that God had been preparing Moses. God had a set time for Moses to be prepared for the task that awaited him.

Be encouraged today and know that whatever your current situation or the process God has you going through, He is preparing you for the ministry that He has called you to do and in His perfect timing it will come to fruition.

NOTES

DAY 32

"Wherefore be ye not unwise but understanding what the will of the Lord is."

-Ephesians 5:17

I often hear people asking, "what is Gods will for my life?" "How can I know?" Perhaps you have asked yourself or someone else these same questions. While I cannot give you step by step instructions for how to achieve Gods plan for you, I can give an overall plan of Gods will for everyone's life. It is Gods will that everyone accept the Lord Jesus Christ as their Savior.

It is Gods will that not one should perish. It is also Gods will that we worship Him with our whole heart, soul and mind. In addition, it is Gods will that we be Baptized with the Holy Spirit and that we receive and exercise the gifts that He blesses us with. It is Gods will that we, in all things, give

Him glory and thanks for all that he has done in our lives. Finally, it is Gods will that we live a life of Holiness.

There are many other things I could mention that are Gods will for our lives, but I think you get the picture. I encourage you today to read the word of God, specifically Romans 12 where it talks about the perfect will of God. Gods word is the instruction book we all need to know and understand the plan of God for our lives.

NOTES

DAY 33

"And there arose a great storm of wind, and the waves beat into the ship, so that it was now full."

-Mark 4:37

This passage of scripture represents the storms of life that we all face at one time or another. Have you ever been in a spiritual storm that you thought would never end? When God allows us to go through circumstances that seem to go on forever, it is for a reason and it is generally for our benefit. Oftentimes God allows storms in our life because He desires to hear from us more.

When things are going well for us, we tend not to pray the way we do when we are going through a storm. Second, God allows storms to test our faith and to show his provision in our lives. God has to allow us to come to a place of not being able to provide for ourselves, not being able to figure things out, so that we can learn how to trust him to provide all that we need.

Be encouraged today knowing that whatever you have need of, God will provide, he will make a way, no matter how impossible the situation seems to you. God knows what to do, when to do it and how to do it.

NOTES

DAY

34

"Turn again, and tell Hezekiah the captain of my people, Thus says the Lord, the God of David your father, I have heard your prayer, I have seen your tears: behold, I will heal you, on the third day you shall go up unto the House of the Lord."

-II Kings 20:5

Hezekiah had begun his reign with the greatest spiritual reforms ever, as well as the blessings of God which would turn his head, causing him to become prideful. He would later turn his face away from all the riches, glory, and grandeur of Judah and Jerusalem, as he saw himself undone, helpless and totally dependent on the mercy of God. With a broken heart Hezekiah would cry out to God and the Lord responded by saying *"I have heard your prayer, I have seen your tears, behold, I will heal you."*

God is no respecter of persons. Whether we are going through the loss of a loved one, a divorce, or the pain that others have a way of inflicting on us, through their words and actions, one thing remains and that is Gods undying love for us. God cares for us and hears the cries of his people.

He sees our hurt and has promised to wipe away every tear that we cry. God is not just the healer of our physical body but also the healer of our broken hearts and emotions. Be encouraged today, knowing that the same words God spoke to Hezekiah, are for us today. Whatever the hurt, whatever the pain, God promises to hear our prayers, wipe away our tears and heal us.

NOTES

DAY 35

"I will bless the Lord at all times: His praise shall continually be in my mouth."

-Psalm 34:1

David is telling us in this scripture, that in every circumstance and at all times, we are to praise the Lord. We have all had those days where everything went wrong or seem to work against us. Those days where the children did not want to cooperate in the morning, you couldn't find your keys, the car wouldn't start and after arriving late to work, the supervisor was waiting to ask you why.

It is at those moments when everything is going wrong that we can choose to call our friends, tell our coworkers how bad our morning has been, or we can just start singing praises to God. Worship is not just for Sunday morning services at Church.

Whether or not you have a beautiful voice does not

matter, just start worshipping God through whatever song you can think of. I once heard a lady say she was having a bad day and the only song she could think of was Jesus loves me and began singing it, suddenly her day began to get better. Be encouraged today in knowing that regardless of the kind of day you are having, it will get better, if you only open your mouth and begin to sing praises unto God. Allow the Holy Spirit to move in your heart and life and glorify Him for who He is and all that he has done for you.

NOTES

DAY 36

"And be found in Him, not having mine own righteousness, which is of the law, but that which is through the faith of Christ, the righteousness which is of God in faith."

-Philippians 3:9

When Jesus died on Calvary's Cross, he fulfilled the Law. It is through the bloodshed of Jesus that we have been made righteous. Our faith should always be exclusively in Him and His finished work at Calvary. It is also through the bloodshed of Jesus at Calvary's cross that we are able, to enter a relationship with Him. To be in relationship with Christ means we recognize, know and can say "I cannot do it in my own strength." We recognize that everything we do for the kingdom of God, is accomplished through Christ helping us and not in our own ability. Oftentimes, we will hear people calling those that attend Church, "religious." Well, I do not know about you, but I for one, am not religious.

There are people who attend church for the purpose of seeing how much they can get done. They make every board meeting a priority, they teach Sunday School, they plan activities, they are busy, busy, busy. However, when it comes to worshipping God, when it comes to giving a second thought to God during the week— they don't, that is religion.

Now, do not get me wrong. There is no harm in working within the Church, providing those good works emanate from our relationship with Christ.

I encourage you today to examine your relationship with Christ. Are you working in the church but never spending time with God? Are you in a relationship with the Lord or are you religious? Good works will not gain you access to Heaven, only a personal relationship with Jesus Christ can do that.

NOTES

DAY 37

"And he said unto me, My grace is sufficient for thee: for my strength is made perfect in weakness. Most gladly therefore will I rather glory in my infirmities, that the power of Christ may rest upon me."

-II Corinthians 12:9

The apostle Paul is said to be the greatest example of Christianity that Christ ever produced. Paul was experiencing some serious problems. We aren't told what issues he was dealing with, however, whatever it was it seemed as though the enemy was trying to kill him.

As Paul was dealing with this problem, he chose to glory in his infirmity so that pride would not come in and intensify the problem. Paul never wanted people to look at him rather than Christ. He wanted others to see Christ in Him as he was going through. Paul cried out to God for him to remove the thorn from his side—to deliver him from the problem. However, God would say to him, "*my grace is sufficient.*"

I have been in that position in my own life, where I have prayed and prayed for God to deliver me from a situation and God said, "*no, my grace is sufficient.*"

Be encouraged today, knowing that no matter what problem you are dealing with, what storm you are in, no matter how much you have prayed for God to take it away, and he hasn't removed it. His grace is sufficient. Rest in Him. He knows best.

NOTES

DAY 38

"Let us hold fast the profession of our Faith without wavering; for He is faithful who promised."

-Hebrews 10:23

The New Covenant promises Salvation and total victory over sin. God is Faithful, His word is truth. When God makes promises to us it is far different than when people make us promises. Gods promises come from the one who said "*I cannot lie.*"

When God promises us something, it may not come instantly, but it will come in his time and according to His will and infinite knowledge. Abraham was promised a son but after many years had passed, and the promise unfulfilled, he took matters into his own hands and as a result, Ishmael was born and caused problems for the promised child, Issac.

Only God has the power to fulfill His promises to us.

Our only responsibility is to believe Him and trust him. Be encouraged today knowing that God is trustworthy and he cannot go against his nature. God is not a man that he should lie. Whatever he has promised you, keep believing him for it. Your blessing is coming through.

NOTES

DAY 39

"Come unto me, all you who labor and are heavy laden, and I will give you rest."

-Mathew 11:28

True rest comes from Jesus Christ and placing our faith in Him. Oftentimes as we go through life, we try to solve our problems on our own. If we have a lost loved one, we say and do everything within our power to try and convert that person. If a problem arises between family or friends, we go out of our way to resolve it.

We wear ourselves down, we worry, we let our problems control us. So many times, we will pray, and lay the problem at the foot of the cross, only to pick it up again. God will let us do all we can, he will allow us to exhaust ourselves in an effort, to bring us to the end of ourselves.

It is at the end of ourselves that we can find Jesus standing there with His arms open, waiting for us to come to Him and give it to him. When we release the problem, then and only then do we enter into his rest. To rest is to say, "okay Lord, I've done all I know to do, I can't do it, please help me." Once we remove our efforts and release that situation to Gods very capable hands, he goes to work on our behalf, and we start to see results.

Be encouraged today knowing that you can release to God what you have fought so hard to try and resolve on your own and He will bring it to pass. He will give you rest.

NOTES

DAY 40

"Who comforteth us in all our tribulation, that we may be able to comfort them which are in any trouble, by the comfort wherewith we ourselves are comforted of God."

-II Corinthians 1:4

As a believer the enemy is constantly pulling at us, coming at us from every direction. He is always speaking lies to us, trying to deceive us, attacking us in our homes, health, finances and spiritually. His goal is to weaken our faith, drag us down and bind us in despair.

At times the enemy will make the world look enticing, to try and distract us and snatch us out of the hand of God. The test of our faith is ongoing, and it can be a daunting task. It seems we are being pushed beyond our human capacity, its as if we do not have the ability to cope with the issues. The truth is, in our own strength we can't stand under the pressure. However, the good news is, we have a comforter. We have the Holy Spirit living on the inside of us, all we have to do, is place our faith in him and His finished work at Calvary. Once we do that, we will know how to receive his comfort. As we find comfort in Christ, we will be able to comfort those around us that are also going through difficult times.

Be encouraged today knowing that no matter how difficult the trial, the comforter dwells on the inside of you and he will surely carry you through. As he carries you through be a blessing to someone else by showing them comfort.

NOTES

DAY 41

"For do I now persuade men, or God? Or do I seek to please men? For if I yet pleased men, I should not be the Servant of Christ."

-Galatians 1:10

Paul having founded the Church of Galatia was writing a letter of indictment to the Church for the amount of false doctrine they were preaching. False prophets and teachers had risen up and perverted the gospel, causing people to leave the message of the cross. Paul became angry at the message being preached to the point of speaking a curse on any man or angel presenting another gospel, other than the message he had presented—the message of the cross.

This should be a lesson to us all. As we go to our prospective churches and sit and listen to teachers, prophets and/or the preacher. What are we hearing? What is being taught? Does it line up with the true word of God? In many of todays Churches they are all about numbers, seeing how many people they can get to fill the pews on Sunday morning. Although, the people may come by the hundreds, what is being taught? Are they being taught sin is wrong, Hell is hot, and the moving of the Holy Spirit is required to have Church and do Gods work? Or are they telling people what they want to hear to keep them coming back.

I encourage you today to ask yourself these questions about the Church you attend. If your answers do not line up with the word of God, then it may be time to move on and find a church that is preaching the cross—the true word of God.

NOTES

DAY 42

"Then He called His twelve disciples together and gave them power and authority over all devils, and to cure diseases."

-Luke 1:9

We are spirit beings and we are constantly living in a spiritual warfare. Everything that comes against us that is not good or of God is Evil and there is a spirit behind it, including sickness. However, just like the disciples, we have been given authority through Jesus Christ and His blood shed at Calvary's Cross, we have been given authority over the powers of darkness, as well as, the authority to lay hands on people and see them healed. Have you ever gone through a season where the enemy attacked you from every angle? Those days when the enemy is putting thoughts in your head nonstop or causing you to worry about things that are never going to happen. We can take authority over the enemy and rebuke him in the name of Jesus. The next time the enemy is coming at you with everything he has, raise up against him and remind him that you do not live by bread alone but by every word that proceeds out of the mouth of God. Remind him who you belong to, stand against him, taking authority over him and watch how fast he will flee.

Be encouraged today knowing that you are not just starting another day, but you are starting your day with authority given to you by God through His son Jesus Christ. Go out today and conquer all that awaits you. You've got this, in Jesus name!

NOTES

DAY 43

"Verily I say unto you, All sins shall be forgiven unto the sons of men, and blasphemies wherewith so ever they shall blaspheme: But he that shall blaspheme against the Holy Ghost hath never forgiveness, but is in danger of eternal damnation: because they said, He hath an unclean spirit."

- Mark 3:28-30

God promises us in His word that when we confess our sins to him, He will be faithful to forgive them and remember them no more as far as the East is from the West. However, often Christians are concerned that they have committed the unpardonable sin of which there is no forgiveness. The unpardonable sin is when one blasphemes the Holy Spirit. An example of this can be found in the book of Mark when the Scribes and Pharisees' knowing Jesus was performing miracles in the power of the Holy Spirit, deliberately gave the credit to Satan in an attempt to discredit the power of the miracles Jesus was performing.

Anyone who blasphemes the Holy Spirit has a hardened heart toward God, rejects God and shows no interest in repenting. One of Satan's tactics he uses against Christians is telling us that we really aren't saved, especially when we fall short and sin against God.

If you are that Christian that worries about whether or not you have committed the unpardonable sin, be encouraged today knowing that the mere fact you are concerned about it, says that you have not blasphemed the Holy Spirit and if you have fallen short and sinned against God, ask Him for forgiveness, he will meet you right where you are, ready to forgive and remember your sins no more.

NOTES

DAY

44

"And they were all filled with the Holy Spirit, and began to speak with other tongues, as the Spirit gave them utterance."

-Acts 2:4

The new covenant contains three baptisms: 1) Baptism into the body of Christ which takes place when we get saved, 2) water baptism that is a witness to others of our new relationship with Jesus Christ and 3) the baptism with the Holy Spirit, when Jesus baptizes the believer into the person of the Holy Spirit.

When a believer is baptized with the with the Holy Spirit the word tells us that the initial evidence will be speaking with other tongues. The purpose of being baptized with the Holy Spirit is to empower the believer with supernatural power for service.

The benefits of being baptized with the Holy Spirit

are endless. We cannot effectively do anything within the kingdom of God without being filled with His power and given his anointing. Many people do not understand what it means to be baptized with the Holy Spirit. Many say it isn't for today's Christian, some say it is of the devil, and others are fearful of it because they do not understand it.

If you are a born-again believer and have not received the baptism of the Holy Spirit, be encouraged today to pray about it, seek Gods face and ask him to fill you and he will. If you want more of God and desire to go to a deeper level in your relationship with God—you can. It's yours for the asking.

NOTES

DAY
45

"My Brethern, count it all joy when you fall into divers temptations; knowing this, that the trying of your Faith works patience. But let patience have her perfect work, that you may be perfect and entire, wanting nothing."

-James 1:2-4

As we go through trials and tribulation, we are to stand on our faith in what God alone can do. God is able to do all things and allows our faith to be tested for the sake of developing patience in us. It is vital to our walk with God that when we go through difficult times, we do not grow discouraged and give up just because we are praying and not hearing from God, not seeing answers to our prayers or our circumstances are not changing, in fact, they may actually be getting worse and will continue to increasingly get worse as we wait on God to move. This act of faith being tested and patience built is not pleasant. It is a very painful process; however, the results are worth it.

Be encouraged today to stay the course, maintain unmovable faith, staying grounded in God and His promises to you. Your ending is going to be better than your beginning and the next time—yes, there will be a next time, you go through the test, you will go through with a higher level of patience than what you had this time.

NOTES

DAY 46

"But they that wait upon the Lord shall renew their strength; they shall mount up with wings as eagles; they shall run, and not be weary; and they shall walk, and not faint."

-Isaiah 40:31

God promises in this verse to strengthen us as we wait upon him. As we wait on the Lord we should seek his face for direction, stay in prayer, constantly being bound together with him. Waiting on the Lord is not always easy. Often, Satan will come at us with everything he's got, to try and move us off the path God has us on.

As humans, we grow impatient, we run to family and friends for advice, which at times can be helpful but we should never take the opinion of others and make decisions for our life. Likewise, we should never assume that what someone else tells us is from God. As believers we also tend to make our own plans and then ask God to bless what we come up with. We label this "*stepping out in faith*". Whatever God has for you, he will show you and he will give you his peace to get through as you wait.

God's desire is total dependency. That means we trust God to guide us and lead us into doing the right thing, at the right time and in his way. We must maintain confidence in God, knowing that he has our best interest in mind. He loves us unconditionally and wants only the best for us.

What have you been believing God for? What area of your life are you waiting for God to move in? Be encouraged today to hold on and rest in Christ while you wait. The answer may not come in the way you think or desire, but the answer will come.

NOTES

DAY

47

"And as he journeyed, he came near Damascus and suddenly there shined around about him a light from Heaven, and he fell to the earth, and heard a voice saying unto him, Saul, Saul, why do you persecute me? And he said, Who are you, Lord?"

-Acts 9:3-5

In this scripture we find Saul on his way to Damascus as he branched out to other cities to persecute the church. On his way to Damascus the appearance of Christ in His Glory came before Saul and the power of God knocked him down. The encounter Saul had with God led to a transformation in him that was so great, he would change his name to Paul. As Paul came to Christ, he realized the error in the direction for which he was headed, and he immediately made the decision to leave behind his old way of living and grasp the new plan God had for his life. Like Paul, we need to learn to let go of the things that were important to us before we accepted Christ. We need to lay down those things in our life that are taking our time away from God. This includes relationships that take too much of our time, causing us not to spend adequate time with God.

Letting go of the things and people that mean so much to us is not easy, but it is imperative that we do it. There is no relationship as important as our relationship with God. I have had to step back and let go of people in my own life. I am not speaking of disowning them, but rather, cutting way back on the time you spend hanging around and communicating with them, that you may spend more time with God.

Be encouraged today, to let go of everything in your life that is taking your time away from God. Get alone with God, in his word, and experience ALL that God has for you as he produces a new life for you to walk in. Lay down the old and pick up the new. Magnify God while setting aside what you desire. The benefits will be well worth it.

NOTES

DAY 48

Let your conversations be without covetousness; and be content with such things as you have: for He has said, I will never leave you, nor forsake you.

-Hebrews 13:5

As Christians we all have our struggles but perhaps the greatest struggle we face at times, is Spiritual. Those times when we go through what man has termed a Spiritual "dry place." It's as though God has left you, never to return. Often during these times, we do not feel like praying, or cannot find the words, reading our Bible is more of a chore than an enjoyment, singing praises to God is like singing our favorite song, there is no worship involved, we do not hear from God because He is being quiet, it is as if God has left us for good.

It is during these times of quietness and feeling nothing

Spiritually that Satan moves in and tells us that we aren't saved, he will, oh so subtly tell us that God has left us and if we aren't strong in our Faith, he will succeed at convincing us of what he is saying.

Satan is a liar! Our God promises us that He will never leave us, nor forsake us! So, be encouraged when you go through a "dry spell" to not give up. Do not base what you are going through on your feelings. Feelings are fickle. They are up and down and all over the place. Press on to keep seeking Gods face and before you know it, He will show up and that spiritual dry spell you found yourself in, will come to a crashing halt.

NOTES

DAY 49

Wherefore come out from among them, and be ye separate, saith the Lord, and touch not the unclean thing and I will receive you.

-II Corinthians 6:17

Does your lifestyle match who you say you are in Christ? A few weeks ago I was having a conversation with an acquaintance of mine when he said to me, "*I am a Christian, I love the Lord but my lifestyle does not match yours Connie.*" He went on to explain that he likes to drink alcohol on occasions, curses at times and enjoys attending events that are non-Christian. My response to him was, "*you say you are a Christian, you say you love the Lord, so ask yourself this question, does your lifestyle match who you say you are in Christ?*" I did not get a reply.

Does your lifestyle match who you say you are in Christ? Is what you say Christ-like or world-like? Is what you watch and listen to Christ-like or world-like? If you go to Church, when you are away from the Church, what are doing and saying?

Do you pray and read your Bible daily? Are you in relationship with God or do you go to Church on Sunday mornings to socialize, ease your conscience because your living like the world the rest of the week? The word of God says to "*Come Out*" from among them (the world) and be ye separate.

We are to be in the world but not living like the world. We are to be a light in the darkness, not hidden in the darkness. I want to encourage you today Christian as you go through your day to ask yourself, is what I'm about to say or do pleasing to God or pleasing to self? Is what I'm about to do of God or of the world? Is my lifestyle matching who I proclaim to be as a Christian?

NOTES

DAY 50

The Lord is their Strength and He is the saving strength of His Anointed.

-Psalm 28:8

There is no other help like the help of God. At times in our life we are going to go through difficult times, circumstances will arise where we have absolutely no control. We find ourselves with our back against the wall and before we know it, we are on our knees with our face buried in the floor and tears flowing as we cry out to God for help. Rest assure, if you have not been in this place to date, the day will come. Loved ones become sick, families fall apart, friends disappoint and hurt us, the stress of the job is more than we can stand or perhaps we find ourselves unemployed by no fault of our own. Life happens and at times Life hits hard. These are all realities that people deal with in one area or the other.

During these times we may feel alone and desperate for answers. Often during these times God will be quiet, because there is a lesson, He desires for us to learn, but it is also during these times of heartache, God carries us. Even though we do not sense His presence, He is there. It seems, we aren't going to make it, yet day after day we are getting up placing one foot in front of the other and moving forward. That is God strengthening us! Be encouraged today and know that no matter what you are facing, dealing with or going through, God is your strength, where you are weak, He is strong. He has everything under control. Seek His face even more and ask Him what lesson He would have you learn as you travel through the storm. He will reveal it to you and as a result you will grow in Him.

NOTES

DAY 51

Even so the tongue is a little member and boast great things. Behold, how great a matter a little fire kindles!

-James 3:5

This scripture tells us that the tongue is a small member of our body, yet it has a powerful influence and is responsible for tremendous things, good and bad alike. James in this scripture is portraying the image of a forest fire starting with only one small spark.

With our tongue, we can create bad, tear down, cause destruction, bring harm to ourselves and others. On the flip side of this, the tongue also has the ability, to lift people up, encourage them, and bless them. It is often said that the physical pain we can cause a person is not as horrendous as the emotional pain we can cause them with our words. We should always be mindful of the words we speak, especially to others.

Be encouraged today to speak kind words to those you come in contact with. Compliment them, encourage them and bless them with your words. Speak to others the way you would have them speak to you and know that by doing so, you are pleasing the Lord Jesus Christ.

NOTES

DAY 52

And they come unto Him, bringing one sick of the palsy, which was borne of four. And when they could not come nigh unto Him for the press, they uncovered the roof where He was: and when they had broken it up, they let down the bed wherein the sick of the palsy lay. When Jesus saw their faith, He said unto the sick of the palsy, Son, thy sins be forgiven thee.

-Mark 2:3-5

In the midst, of the storms of life, have you ever wanted to just give up and quit? Have the circumstances ever been so overwhelming and looked so impossible that the only way out seemed to be to give up? I'm sure as Christians we have all felt this way at one time or the other. In this scripture Jesus had just returned to Capernaum after weeks of ministering around the area of Galilee. He arrived at the home of Peter, one of His soon-to-be disciples, as noise of His return spread throughout the city. As a result, hundreds of people began to descend on Peter's home, and it soon filled to capacity. In the crowd was a man who had been paralyzed for many years, lying on a cot. This man was unable to move and do for himself and as a result, he was dependent on others for everything he needed.

He was not only afflicted in his physical body but Spiritually he was without God. Depending on those helping him to move him from place to place, after he, as well as, the men carrying him, heard that Jesus was in the city, the men did all they could to get their paralyzed friend to Jesus so he could receive his miracle, believe and get saved. These men stopped at nothing to get their friend to Jesus and when they couldn't get through the crowd and the press, they managed to get him to the top of the house, remove the roof and lower him down.

These men faced an impossible situation and they could have given up, but they didn't. They were determined to get their friend to Jesus, and they did. Be encouraged today not to give up. No matter what problems you are facing or how impossible your circumstances may be, stay focused on Jesus and what He can do to solve them, let your determination keep you pressing on in your walk with God and stay in the fight, determined to make it to the end!

NOTES

DAY 53

And Sarai said unto Abram, behold now, the Lord has restrained me from bearing: I pray you, go in unto my maid; it may be that I may obtain children by her. And Abram hearkened to the voice of Sarai.

-Genesis 16:2

In this scripture Abram (Abraham) and Sarai grow impatient after God has promised them a child and they have yet to conceive. Sarai tells Abram to go and lay with her maid, Hagar. Abram did as Sarai had instructed him to do, rather than waiting on the Lord and His timing.

At times in our life God will make us promises, show us things that He has for us but often there is a delay in receiving what God has promised. Like Abraham and Sarai, we grow impatient and take matters into our own hands, instead of waiting on God for direction. The worse thing we can do is get ahead of God and try to force what only God can do in our lives. God wants us to trust him and His timing. God has a set time for everything.

God promises us a renewed strength to keep trusting Him as we wait. Regardless of how long you have been waiting on God and for His promise to you, be encouraged today to keep seeking Gods face for wisdom, guidance and direction. Do not take matters into your own hands, your promise is on the way.

NOTES

DAY 54

Peace I leave with you, My peace I give unto you: not as the world giveth, give I unto you. Let not your heart be troubled, neither let it be afraid.

-John 14:27

If you have accepted Jesus Christ as your Lord and Savior, then you should have peace in your heart. We receive peace in our hearts the moment we received Christ into our hearts. Jesus paid a high price with the giving of His life at Calvary's Cross for us to be able to receive and maintain peace. So, what is the peace of God? It is an inner calmness, quietness, and fortitude that He puts in our inner being through Jesus Christ. The same way we received the peace of God, we walk in it, and live in it, by Faith. Satan will fight you tooth and nail for your peace. The times we are living in, have reached a new level of crazy. If we get caught up into the things of this world and turn our eyes from God for even a second, we are in trouble. The enemy will move in and try to steal our peace. If we watch too much secular television or listen to music that is not spirit filled Christian music, or read material that is not of God, we are letting the world in and too much of the world equals, not enough time with God, which equals—no peace.

Be encouraged today to spend time with God before you start your day, during your lunch break and at the end of your day. Guard your heart and mind from anything Satan can use to come in and steal your peace. Rest in Christ and let His peace carry you through the day.

NOTES

DAY 55

And when He had called unto Him his Twelve Disciples, He gave them power against unclean spirits, to cast them out, and to heal all manner of sickness and all manner of disease.

-Matthew 10:1

Jesus was on a mission to see souls saved, people healed and delivered. During His ministry He called on Twelve Disciples to help Him carry out the task at hand. Likewise, we have been called as children of God to do His work. Every single believer has a call on his or her life to do something for the kingdom of God. Some are called to Evangelize, some to teach, some to Pastor, some to lead praise and worship, some to keep nursery and the list goes on. However, regardless of the title we carry as a disciple for Christ, we have all been called to see souls saved. We are to witness to people and live a lifestyle that witnesses to the people around us. If you are unable to get out and be a direct witness to someone, then you can support a Church or ministry that is preaching the Cross and reaching the lost. By supporting them with your prayers and finances, you are being an instrumental part in winning every soul to Christ that surrenders to Him through their efforts.

Be encouraged today to go out and fulfill the mission God has called you to do. Tell someone about Jesus today and the price He paid for them to be spared an eternal Hell and to be able to live a life of peace and joy. In doing so you will in return be rewarded by your Father in Heaven.

NOTES

DAY

56

Finally, my brethren, be strong in the Lord, and in the power of his might. Put on the whole armour of God, that you may be able to stand against he wiles of the Devil. For we wrestle not against flesh and blood, but against principalities, against powers, against the rulers of the darkness of this world, against spiritual wickedness in high places. Wherefore take unto you the whole armour of God, that you may be able to withstand in the evil day, and having done all, to stand. Stand therefore.

-Ephesians 6:10-14

According to Websters Dictionary the meaning of the word wrestle is *"to contend by grappling with and striving to trip or throw an opponent down or off balance."* The wrestling match we are in as mentioned in this scripture, is not against another human being, in fact, it's not against flesh and blood at all but rather against the powers of darkness. We wrestle with Satan as we enter a daily Spiritual warfare. So, how do we wrestle with the powers of darkness that stand stronger and more powerful than us, waiting to take us out? The first way, as I mentioned in a previous devotion, is to learn to rest in Christ. Be secure in Him and what He died for you to have. Maintain your peace. The second way is to Praise the Lord with all your heart, soul and mind, just open your mouth and start singing and worshipping the Lord. Third, stay in the word of God and let it strengthen you.

Be encouraged today in all that you do, to just simply rest and praise the Lord through worship. Put on the whole armour of God, standing strong in Jesus Christ and His finished work at Calvary. Doing so will send the enemy packing. He is no match for Jesus Christ or who you are in Christ!

NOTES

DAY 57

And unto the Angel of the Church of the Laodiceans write; These things says the Amen, the faithful and true witness, the beginning of the creations of God. I know your works, that you are neither cold nor hot: I would you were cold or hot. So then because you are lukewarm, and neither cold nor hot, I will spue you out of my mouth.

-Revelation 3:14-16

We are currently living in Revelation Chapter three. The Church today is the Laodicean church talked about in the above scripture. The Bible is no longer honored as it once was in past years. The majority of Americans do not follow Godly principles found in the word of God and have laid it down, never to open it again.

Christians do not understand the content of the word

of God, primarily because the truth is not being taught from behind our pulpits. So called Pastors have replaced the true word of God with what people want to hear. Sin is no longer being preached in most churches, but rather people are being told to live the way they choose, because after all, they are covered by Grace. Grace is NOT a license to sin! In addition, our Government officials are doing all they can to take away the rights and religious freedom of Pastors and Christians who are preaching the truth and continue to stand for God.

Be encouraged today to face persecution head on and to defend your Religious Freedoms and Church, if your Pastor is preaching the word of God in its entirety. If you are not in a Faith based church that preaches the truth, then find one that does. Do not let the Laodicean church lead you to an eternal Hell.

NOTES

DAY 58

And God said let there be light: and there was light.

-Genesis 1:3

God said! We see in this short verse how God spoke, and it was done. We can learn a lot from this scripture. As Christians we have a target on our back and Satan is relentless in his efforts to hit it. Even as I write this our Nation is shut down due to COVID-19, leaving many unemployed, losing loved ones to the COVID-19 virus, our Churches are closed, and people are living under a Spirit of fear. In spite of all that is currently taking place in our world and all that we have to endure in this life, God is in control! He, in His infinite wisdom, knows best and with just one word from our Lord the hardship you are facing as well as COVID-19 will go away just as quickly as it came.

Be encouraged today knowing that the God who spoke the universe into existence is still on the throne. He has not given us a spirit of fear, so choose today not to live a life of fear but one of faith and of a sound mind.

NOTES

DAY 59

Bless the Lord, You his angels, that excel in strength, that do his commandments, hearkening unto the voice of his word.

-Psalm 103:20

Angels are mentioned all throughout the Bible. The number of angels God created is unknown, but the Bible tells us that there are "ten thousand times ten thousand, and thousands of thousands." God created them to be messengers for him and ministers to man. In addition, the Bible tells us that angels were sent by God to believers to provide help, deliver specific messages and, at times, they were commanded to destroy.

Once we received the Lord Jesus Christ into our hearts and became a believer, we were assigned an angel. Yes. We have an angel with us everywhere we go, watching over us and keeping us. *"Are they not all ministering spirits, sent forth* *to minister for them who shall be heirs of salvation?" (*Heb.1:14) It's important to remember that angels are given charge over us by God and that they follow His command. They are not to be worshipped, put before God, or to take His place in our lives. They merely go with us at Gods command to warn, rescue from danger, deliver and strengthen us to resist temptation.

Be encouraged today to face the day head on, knowing that "*the one*" Christ Jesus goes before you, the Holy Spirit is covering you and Gods assigned angel is protecting you.

NOTES

DAY

60

For by Grace are you saved through faith; and that not of yourselves: It is the Gift of God: Not of works, lest any man should boast.

-Ephesians 2:8-9

It is by Grace through faith that an individual is saved. Joining a Church, being baptized in water and good works will not save you. Today, I encourage you to accept the Lord Jesus Christ as your savior and experience the peace and life of joy that only comes from Him. If you have never said the sinners prayer believing in your heart that Jesus died on Calvary's Cross for you and three days later rose from the grave and now sits at the right hand of the Father making intercession for us all, then today is your day. Just say the following prayer and believe in your heart and you will be saved.

"Dear God in Heaven, I come to you today as a lost sinner."

"I am asking you that you save my soul and cleanse me from all sin." "I realize in my heart my need of salvation, which can only come through Jesus Christ." "I am accepting Christ into my heart and what He did on the Cross in order to purchase my redemption." "In obedience to your word, I confess with my mouth the Lord Jesus, and believe in my heart that God has raised Him from the dead." "You have said in your word that whosoever calls on the name of the Lord will be saved." "I have called upon your name as you have said, and I believe that right now, I am saved."

NOTES

ABOUT THE AUTHOR

A current resident of Gates County, North Carolina, Connie Smithson also worked in the rural County for years as a Social Worker. She graduated from College of the Albemarle with an Associates of Arts Degree, as well as Elizabeth City State with a Bachelor of Science degree in Criminal Justice and Kaplan University with a Master's degree in Criminal Justice. Today, Connie is working to serve God in every capacity of life. She has dedicated her life to following God's lead as He opens doors for her to go into the world and encourage others with her testimony of God's healing power and saving grace. It's Connie's hope that through her book people will be encouraged as they go through the hardships of life and come to understand that the light at the end of the trial is brighter than the darkness they walked through during the trial.

Connie is available to speak where God sends her. For more information, please contact:

E-mail: d854@hotmail.com

Printed in the United States
By Bookmasters